DON'T MESS WITH ME

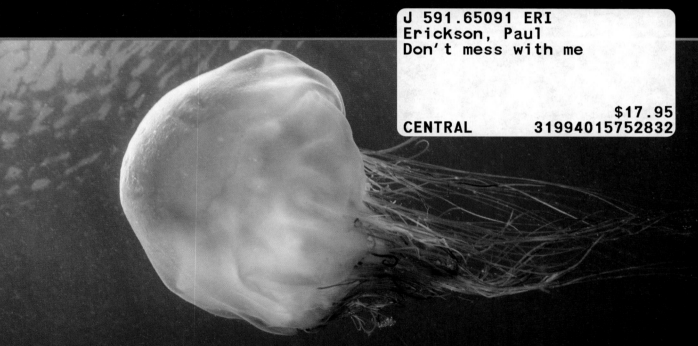

The Strange Lives of Venomous Sea Creatures

PAUL ERICKSON

Photography by Andrew Martinez

TILBURY HOUSE PUBLISHERS, THOMASTON, MAINE

To Susan—life companion, adventurer, and dive buddy. —P.E.

To Candace, my best friend and wife. —A.M.

Tilbury House Publishers
12 Starr Street
Thomaston, Maine 04861
800-582-1899 • www.tilburyhouse.com

First edition: December 2018 • 10 9 8 7 6 5 4 3 2 1

ISBN 978-0-88448-551-3

Library of Congress Control Number: 2018956505

Cover and interior design by Frame25 Productions
Printed in the United States via Four Colour Print Group

Acknowledgments

Thanks to Dr. Paul Greenwood, Dr. Roy Caldwell, and J. Michael McIntosh, MD for their kind assistance with fact checking and expertise.

Photo Credits

Photos are by Andrew Martinez except as follows: p.5 top, Ned DeLoach / www.fishid.com · p.11 sidebar, ER Degginger / Science Source · p.14 bottom inset, Alberto Loyo / Shutterstock · p.16 top left, ANT Photo Library / Science Source · p.16 top center, Dennis Kunkel Microscopy / Science Source · p.16 top right, ANT Photo Library / Science Source · p.18 top, LauraDin / iStock · p.19 top left, Michael McCoy / Science Source · p.19 top right, Franco Banfi / Science Source · p.20 top right, Solodov Aleksei / Shutterstock · p.20 sidebar, Paul Erickson · pages 22 and 23, Thomas M. Iliffe, Texas A&M University at Galveston · p.33 top, orlandin / Shutterstock · p.33 inset, bulente-vren / Shutterstock · p.37 top, W. Leo Smith, University of Kansas Biodiversity Institute · pp.38 – 39 main image, RibeirodosSantos / iStock

DON'T BE FOOLED.

BLUE-RINGED OCTOPUS
Timid but Deadly

A blue-ringed octopus grabs a crab dinner off Bali, Indonesia.

DON'T MESS!

Timid and reclusive except when feeding, the greater blue-ringed octopus glides across coral reefs in the waters of Sri Lanka, Australia, New Guinea, Indonesia, the Philippines, and southern Japan. Measuring less than 8 inches (20 cm) from arm tip to arm tip, this little animal can kill a person with its venomous bite. It eats shrimp, small crabs, bivalve mollusks, and fish and tries to avoid being eaten by moray eels, some of which appear to be immune to the toxin.

The colors of a blue-ringed octopus intensify with excitement as the predator reaches around a rock to attack a crab.

IS THAT THING POISONOUS OR VENOMOUS?
(They're Not the Same)

Most of the 120 species of pufferfish—including this star pufferfish—contain the deadly nerve poison tetrodotoxin.

Lots of animals depend more on chemical weapons than on teeth, claws, speed, or strength for survival, but not all of them are venomous. The Japanese pufferfish, for example, carries a powerful toxin in its liver and other organs. This animal chemist is extremely poisonous—and would-be predators avoid it for that reason—but it is not venomous.

To be venomous, an animal must be able to *inject* its toxins into other living

As in other pufferfish, the nerve poison in the skin and liver of a scribbled or map pufferfish varies from season to season and place to place.

The toxic cocktails of most venomous sea creatures include proteins and peptides (small-chain proteins). Some of these toxins disrupt the functioning of their victims' vital nerves and muscles. Others attack the circulatory system: blood cells, blood vessels, and the heart. Some cause extreme pain, while others do their damage painlessly.

HOW NATURE WORKS

WHY BE VENOMOUS?

Any trait that helps an organism live longer and reproduce more successfully is more likely to be passed down to later generations. That's how natural selection works. And acting over multiple generations, natural selection causes new species to evolve.

Venom production has evolved in many species, so it must have advantages. Does it require less energy than fighting, fleeing, or chasing? Maybe so—and an animal that uses less energy to survive can keep more calories in reserve to look for mates, produce eggs, and feed and protect its young. Scientists are still trying to sort out this energy equation.

NORTHERN RED ANEMONE
Beautiful Stinger

A spiny, indigestible-looking green sea urchin meets a flowery, delicate-looking northern red anemone, and then the anemone swallows the urchin. There isn't much plot development in this story, but it has a surprise ending!

In the cold North Atlantic Ocean, a spiny green sea urchin roams across a rocky reef toward an immobile anemone. Will the urchin's spines puncture and kill the soft-bodied anemone?

Nope. Instead, when the urchin is close enough, the anemone spears it with venom-filled threads. The paralyzed urchin soon dies, and the anemone swallows its prickly meal whole, spines and all. After digesting the urchin's soft parts, it spits out the spines and shell. Mmmm, good!

DON'T MESS!

Anemones and their closest relatives, including stinging sea jellies and corals, are members of a big group of animals called cnidaria (nye-DAIR-ee-uh; the "c" is silent). Cnidarians appeared in the sea about 600 million years ago and were probably the first venomous animals to evolve on Earth. The anemone's fingerlike tentacles are armed with thousands of special cells called cnidocytes (NYE-doe-sites). Each cnidocyte

contains an organelle called a nematocyst (nem-AT-oh-sist), some of which can sting.

Powered by water pressure, stinging nematocysts shoot microscopic, hollow, venom-filled threads at astonishingly high speeds. The threads can pierce a sea urchin's shell. An anemone can kill fish, shrimp, crabs, sea jellies, zooplankton, and even other anemones this way—quite an accomplishment for an animal that has no bones, armor, teeth, or even much ability to move.

The northern red anemone normally can't sting people, because our skin is too thick. Instead, the nematocysts triggered by touching this species feel sticky. But other anemones sting people severely, which is one reason divers wear protective wetsuits even in warm water.

Completely discharged nematocyst

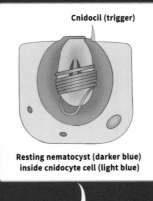

Cnidocil (trigger)

Resting nematocyst (darker blue) inside cnidocyte cell (light blue)

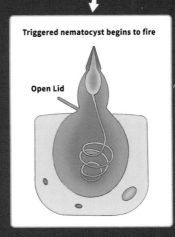

Triggered nematocyst begins to fire

Open Lid

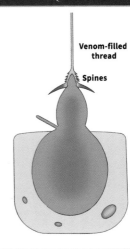

Venom-filled thread

Spines

ANIMAL PARTNERS
Clownfish and Anemones

Small and defenseless, clownfish need protection from
ocean predators, and they
find it among the tentacles
of tropical anemones.

How do the little fish avoid getting
stung and eaten by their bodyguards? There
may be a chemical agent in a clownfish's slimy mucus
coating that prevents the anemone from sensing
the fish as prey. More investigation is needed to solve this mystery.

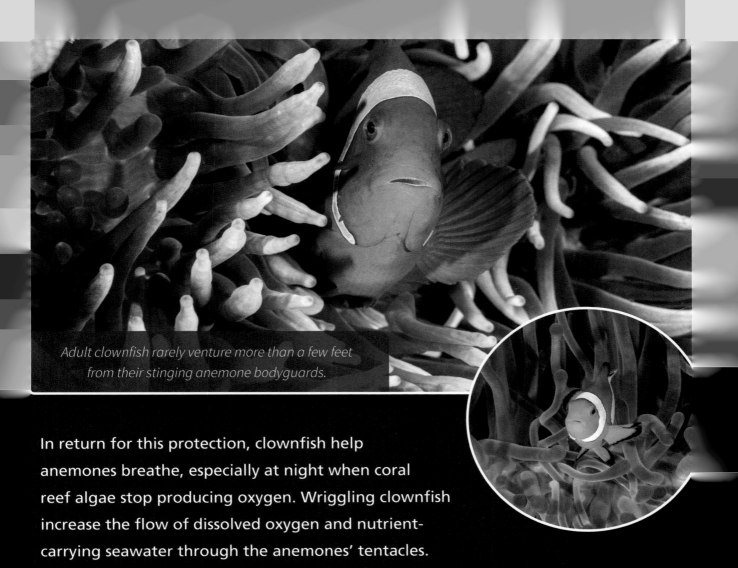

Adult clownfish rarely venture more than a few feet from their stinging anemone bodyguards.

In return for this protection, clownfish help anemones breathe, especially at night when coral reef algae stop producing oxygen. Wriggling clownfish increase the flow of dissolved oxygen and nutrient-carrying seawater through the anemones' tentacles.

HOW NATURE WORKS

STINGERS IN THE CLASSROOM

Many students meet their first venomous aquatic animal when they study the hydra in biology class. Although this freshwater cnidarian can't sting you, it uses its tentacles armed with stinging nematocysts to paralyze tiny zooplankton, which it then eats.

STAR CORAL
Stinging Stones

Halloween decorations? No. These are coral polyps with central mouths and surrounding tentacles in full view.

When night falls over a coral reef off the coast of Belize in Central America, swarms of tiny zooplankton called copepods rise from the Caribbean depths to feed in the shallow waters of the reef. Each copepod—a crustacean related to shrimp but less than a tenth of an inch (2 mm) long—is shaped like a fat rice grain with a rigid tail, two long antennae up front, and a single dark eyespot.

Relative to their size, copepods are among the fastest animals on Earth, able to move 500 times their body length in less than a second. The tiny creatures occasionally blunder into the venomous tentacles of a coral polyp—an animal no bigger than the tip of your smallest finger that occupies a cavity within a five-foot-wide (1.5 m) dome-shaped star coral colony.

A colony of star coral polyps with tentacles retracted.

Tentacles extended to feed.

Like its close cousins the sea anemones, the coral polyp fires stinging nematocysts into copepods contacting its tentacles, injecting venom that almost instantly immobilizes the prey. The crustaceans die and are digested in the polyp's primitive stomach-like cavity.

HOW NATURE WORKS

ANIMAL ARCHITECTURE

Most stony corals, including the star coral, are colonies of individual polyps. Each polyp extracts chemicals from seawater to build a protective limestone cup around its soft body. Neighboring cups cement themselves together to form a colony.

Coral colonies are among the largest and oldest structures built by living things. Only the surface of the colony is alive; this living layer sits atop many older layers of dead coral. It's like a modern city built atop the remains of ancient civilizations. Stony corals form reef systems hundreds of miles long.

The colonies are living greenhouses, getting much of their food from zooxanthellae—single-celled dinoflagellates (*Symbiodinium*) living inside the polyps' soft tissues. During daylight hours, these algae cells

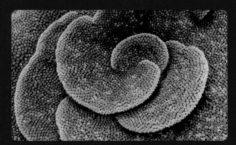

Many stony coral colonies grow in shapes that expose the zooxanthellae in the polyps to sunlight.

use the sun's energy to manufacture food by photosynthesis, just as land plants do. Much of the food leaks out of the zooxanthellae and is absorbed by the coral.

LION'S MANE SEA JELLY
Venomous Drifter

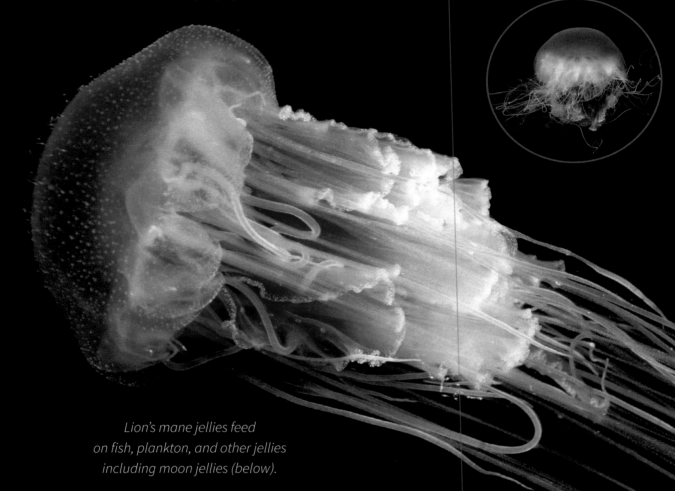

Lion's mane jellies feed on fish, plankton, and other jellies including moon jellies (below).

Like an extraterrestrial mothership, the reddish-orange disc of a lion's mane jelly some three feet (0.9 meter) in diameter descends slowly and silently through a cold, dark, North Atlantic bay near midnight. Tiny bioluminescent planktonic organisms twinkle like a million stars in the surrounding waters.

nearly 20 feet (6 meters) below the disc, are loaded for action.

Below the lion's mane drifts a squadron of ten smaller, clear, disc-shaped moon jellies. The descending curtain of tentacles envelopes the moon jellies almost imperceptibly, and stinging nematocysts inject the prey with venom. Like a slow-motion sci-fi tractor beam, the tentacles transport the entire squadron of immobilized animals to the mouth of the mothership to be devoured.

DON'T MESS!

Sea jellies have been around for hundreds of millions of years. How have these thin-skinned drifters lacking a complex nervous system and strong muscles survived in oceans full of hungry animals with claws, beaks, and teeth? A sea jelly's venom-packed stingers let it catch and immobilize live fish before the fish can bite and tear the jelly to pieces.

In Arthur Conan Doyle's novel *The Adventure of the Lion's Mane*, detective Sherlock Holmes and his companion, Dr. Watson, discover that the killer of a swimmer found dead on a rocky shore was not, after all, a human, but a lion's mane. In reality, it is unlikely that a lion's mane could kill a strong swimmer in good health, but its stings are painful.

THE UPSIDE-DOWN SEA JELLY

The upside-down jelly inverts itself to expose its internal symbiotic microalgae to more sunlight for photosynthesis.

Upside-down sea jellies live, well, upside down, on and above sandy bottoms in warm seas. Merely approaching one can cause it to release unseen nematocysts into the water around it. The stingers feel prickly on unprotected skin but are not dangerous to humans. Like many corals, this animal houses single-celled algae (*Symbiodinium*) in its tissues, and it is often mistaken for a patch of seaweed.

BOX JELLY
Danger Down Under

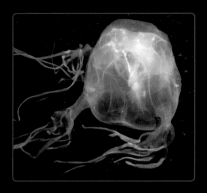

Box jellies grow up to 12 inches (30 cm) in diameter. The animals have four eye clusters, each consisting of six primitive eyes.

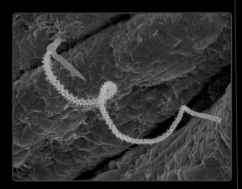

A scanning electron micrograph of an ejected box jelly nematocyst shows the barbed end that injects venom into the prey.

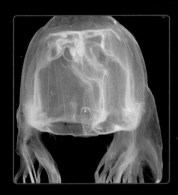

This box jelly (also known as a sea wasp) in Australian waters shows the animal's four-cornered shape.

An American tourist, thrilled to have left behind a northern hemisphere winter for summer in North Queensland, Australia, jogs across a pristine sandy beach toward the inviting sea, but stops when an agitated lifeguard sprints toward him. The lifeguard points toward a nearby sign warning swimmers about sea jellies. An encounter with a box jelly can kill a swimmer.

His enthusiasm dampened, the tourist is happy to learn of a safe swimming area farther down the beach, where a wall of jelly-excluding netting hangs to the seafloor from a floating boom. Lifeguards watch for any stray jellies that might somehow enter the sting-free zone.

DON'T MESS!

Also in Australian waters, the tiny and barely visible Irukandji box jelly causes extremely painful and often long-lasting symptoms in people stung by it. The jelly is named after a group of indigenous people in the Australian province of North Queensland.

CHINESE DRAGON SEA SLUG
Stealing Stingers

A slug glides slowly across a coral reef in the Philippine Islands, browsing as it goes. The little animal, not quite three inches (7 cm) long, does not detect the hungry wrasse—a reef fish—behind it. The slug looks like a soft, fleshy delicacy to the fish, which opens its mouth and takes a tentative taste. But in the next moment the wrasse spits its prey back out again and moves swiftly away. The sea slug lives this day.

Like stony corals, the Chinese dragon sea slug harbors photosynthetic zooxanthellae in its tissues, contributing to the color variations this species displays.

The tiny venomous hydroids the slug has been eating have saved its life. When a slug eats hydroids—animals related to sea anemones—the slug itself is not stung. Instead, it transports the hydroids' microscopic, venom-packed stinging nematocysts from its mouth to the tips of the frilly structures on its back. Apparently, the stolen stingers irritate the mouths of small fish that nibble on the slug.

CONE SNAILS
Venomous Night Crawlers

A textile cone snail hunting by night, with its proboscis visible beneath the siphon.

Around midnight, a cone snail crawls at a snail's pace across a sandy bottom in the tropical waters of the Fiji Islands.

Though it looks as harmless as a garden snail, it is a formidable hunter. Catching the scent of a nearby fish through its siphon, the snail approaches its prey.

When it is close enough, the snail extends a tube called a proboscis toward the fish. The tube contains a tiny, venomous dart shaped remark-

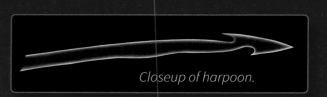

Closeup of harpoon.

ably like the harpoons once used by whalers. When the proboscis touches the fish, water pressure propels the harpoon through the victim's scales and skin. Instantly, powerful neurotoxins paralyze the fish, which the snail eats alive.

A cone snail attacking a strawberry conch in the Solomon Islands.

This cone snail extends its siphon to draw fresh seawater to its gills and sense the chemical traces of prey. The deadly proboscis is retracted for now. Its two tiny eyes, on stalks peek out beneath the siphon and above the animal's fleshy foot. The eyes detect light and shadows but not precise images.

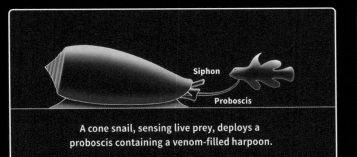

Siphon

Proboscis

A cone snail, sensing live prey, deploys a proboscis containing a venom-filled harpoon.

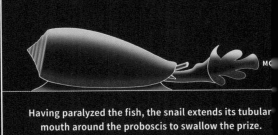

Having paralyzed the fish, the snail extends its tubular mouth around the proboscis to swallow the prize.

OW NATURE
WORKS

MEDICINES FROM CONE SNAIL VENOM

One of the scientists using cone snail venom to develop new pain-relieving drugs is Baldamero Olivera, who encountered cone snails while growing up in the Philippines. While working in Olivera's laboratory at the University of Utah, Michael McIntosh, barely out high school, discovered a peptide in the venom of a *Conus magus* (magician's cone snail). Called ziconotide (brand-name Prialt), and synthesized in a laboratory, it is the first painkilling d inspired by a cone snail venom.

McIntosh believes that biochemists have barely begun to tap the medicinal potential cone snail venom. There are an estimated 500 species of venomous cone snails, each of wh may have as many as 100 chemicals in its venom worth investigating as potential medicin

BLOODWORM
The Bait Bites Back

Amphipods like this are frequent bloodworm prey.

On the coast of Maine, in a mudflat exposed at low tide, a 10-inch (25 cm) predatory bloodworm—a relative of the harmless earthworm—slithers through its dark, slippery, subsurface world. The worm is aptly named; the blood-red color of the iron compound hemoglobin (also present in human blood) is visible through its thin skin.

Nearby, a half-inch-long (13 mm) crustacean called an amphipod shelters inside a J-shaped burrow it has dug into the mud. With lightning speed, the bloodworm fires its fleshy proboscis out of its mouth. Four hooked fangs on the end of the proboscis snare the amphipod and inject venom into it. Then the proboscis retracts, dragging the paralyzed amphipod into the worm's maw to be devoured.

DON'T MESS!

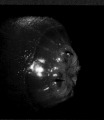

Worm harvesters working in mudflats on the northeast coast of North America know how valuable bloodworms are as bait for recreational fishing. They also know that when handled carelessly, the bloodworm can deliver a bite as painful as a bee sting. A venom delivery system must be as effective as the venom itself, which is why the fangs of a bloodworm contain copper. This durable metal helps the sharp fangs from wearing out as the worm moves through mud and sand.

BEARDED FIREWORM
Bristling with Spines

Two divers—a student and his instructor—are exploring a coral reef in the Caribbean Sea. Just below them, the student notices a brilliantly colored worm creeping across a pile of dead coral rubble. He extends a hand toward the worm, but his instructor quickly grabs his arm, then makes the diver's two-fisted, arms-across-the-chest danger signal.

The delicate venom-containing bristles on this fireworm provide effective protection from browsing fish and other predators.

The colorful creature is a fireworm, and it can sting. Its defensive arrays of tiny, fragile, hollow bristles filled with venom break off on contact with an intruder. Then, like shards of broken glass, the bristles penetrate skin, allowing venom to enter the wounds. The result can be severe irritation—enough to deter a browsing predator or a curious diver from messing around with this creature.

BLIND REMIPEDE

Danger in the Dark

Deep in the maze-like recesses of an undersea cave, it is as dark as a moonless night all day long. There, a tiny, blind, venomous crustacean called a remipede senses the motion of a nearby shrimp and attacks it.

First, the remipede immobilizes the shrimp by injecting a neurotoxic venom through a pair of front claws. Next, it shoots enzymes into the shrimp that liquefy the victim's insides. Then the attacker slurps up its nutritious smoothie.

A scanning electron microscope (SEM) photo of a remipede's fangs.

THE FIRST KNOWN
VENOMOUS CRUSTACEAN

Until 1981, none of the animals known as crust
ceans—a group of some 70,000 species includir
shrimp, crabs, and lobsters—was considered ver
omous. Then, in the Bahama Islands, highly traine
divers exploring an underwater cave connected
the sea discovered this blind venomous remipede

FLOWER AND FIRE
Venomous Sea Urchins

Each of the many flower-like pedicellariae with purple centers covering this flower urchin conceals three venomous fangs.

Some sea urchins, such as the flower urchin of the Western Pacific Ocean, put up a strong defense against would-be predators.

Close-up of a fire urchin showing spines with venomous tips.

A shrimp on a fire urchin.

Sticking out from this animal's body are tiny pincers called pedicellariae, which help the urchin rid its shell of parasites, algae, and debris. What's unusual about the flower urchin is that each of these pincers is tipped with three venomous fangs capable of repelling urchin-eating triggerfish.

A tiny crab shelters amid fire urchin spines.

Another venomous sea urchin, the fire urchin, has tiny, venom-containing bulbs on its spines. Shrimp and crabs find safety among the spines, much as clownfish shelter themselves amid an anemone's tentacles.

CROWN OF THORNS SEA STAR

Touch Me Not!

As striking as a multicolored fire urchin may be, there are few sea creatures as eye-catching as sea stars. Touching a harmless sea star in a tidal pool is often our first introduction to marine biology.

But no one should touch the sea star called the crown of thorns. The arm span of a large specimen can reach 20 inches (51 cm). This armored beast prowls over and eats live coral while defending itself with hundreds of long, sharp spines, each of which is coated with a layer of venomous skin called epithelium.

When a spine punctures the skin of an unfortunate fish or diver, the epithelium enters the puncture wound, causing pain and destroying blood cells.

BLUESPOTTED STINGRAY
Passive Protection

At the edge of Egypt's Sinai Desert, 50 feet (15 m) under the waves of the Red Sea, a bluespotted ray rests on the sandy seabed. This close relative of sharks is shy and non-aggressive unless it is devouring small crabs, shrimp, and fish.

TAIL
SPINES

Like sharks, stingrays have flexible cartilage—as in human ears and noses—in place of bones.

DINNER AT THE STINGRAY DINER

HOW NATURE WORKS

Stingray venom is extremely potent, perhaps because seawater washes away much of the venom from a wound, much as water from a faucet cleanses a cut finger. Even a trace of the ray's venom is painful, but that is sometimes not enough. One great hammerhead shark was caught with nearly 100 stingray spines embedded in its mouth. Apparently, a hungry hammerhead will tolerate a very sore palate in exchange for a seafood delicacy.

But when a scalloped hammerhead shark approaches, its terrible toothed mouth open to kill, the ray undergoes a ferocious transformation. It suddenly thrusts its tail upward and impales the shark with a pair of venomous tail spines. The spines' venom-containing sheath inflicts instant and intense pain in the shark, which breaks off the attack and swims away.

The barbs on a stingray spine anchor the weapon in the victim's flesh while venom enters the wound.

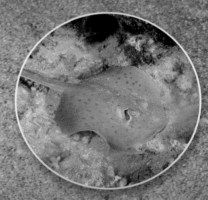

The opening just behind the ray's yellow eye is a spiracle. By drawing water through these dorsal (top) openings, the fish is able to breathe without getting its gills clogged with sand.

HOW NATURE WORKS

SWORDFIGHT WITH A STINGRAY

As the tale is told, in the year 1608, in the Chesapeake Bay, the famed Captain John Smith was stung in the wrist by a stingray while spearing fish with his sword. Although he became ill, he turned the ray into a seafood dinner.

SCORPIONFISH
All in the Family

Spiny devilfish.

Paddle-flap scorpionfish.

Ambon scorpionfish.

Weedy scorpionfish.

Another weedy scorpionfish.

Several of the most dangerous venomous fishes
in the oceans belong to the scorpionfish family
(Scorpenidae), which includes a variety of species resem-
bling goblins, gargoyles, and seaweed-covered rocks.

Each of the family members shown here features a stout
body with fixed, venom-injecting spines on the animal's back
(dorsal) spines and often on other fins. Like many stingrays,
most of the species in this family rest on the bottom between
occasional brief swims. Frilly skin and astonishingly effective coloration make them invisible to predators and prey, camouflaged as algae,
sponges, corals, and debris.

*Tasseled scorpionfish
resting on a coral in
the Philippines.*

3

REEF STONEFISH
Don't Tread on Me

This is the most dangerous member of the scorpionfish family. It's easy to mistake a camouflaged stonefish for a piece of dead coral covered with sponges and algae, and the venom delivered by the dorsal spines can be fatal to people unlucky enough to step on one. The camouflaged fish waits in ambush, snapping up unsuspecting victims with its cavernous mouth.

Perhaps the winner of the world ugly fish contest—or at least a runner-up—the stonefish looks so much like its surroundings that smart divers know to keep their hands off the coral reefs where it lives.

PALETTE SURGEONFISH
Venomous Switchblades

A palette surgeonfish in the sea off Indonesia.

Surgeonfish are a family of active swimmers that use venom to defend themselves. When threatened, the palette surgeonfish erects scalpel-like spines connected to venom glands. Whipping its tail from side to side, it cuts and stings other fish that get too close. (A scalpel is a small knife used by surgeons during medical procedures—thus, the name surgeonfish.)

The paired spines located on both sides of the fish's body project from the front end of a bright yellow triangular tail patch. The prominent yellow shape is a warning sign saying DON'T MESS WITH ME!

HOW NATURE WORKS

BRIGHT WARNING COLORS

Aposematic coloration refers to any bold color pattern that advertises its bearer's ability to cause serious discomfort—or worse—to a predator. Aposematic colorations range from the bold black and white stripes of a skunk to the bright yellow tail patch on a surgeonfish.

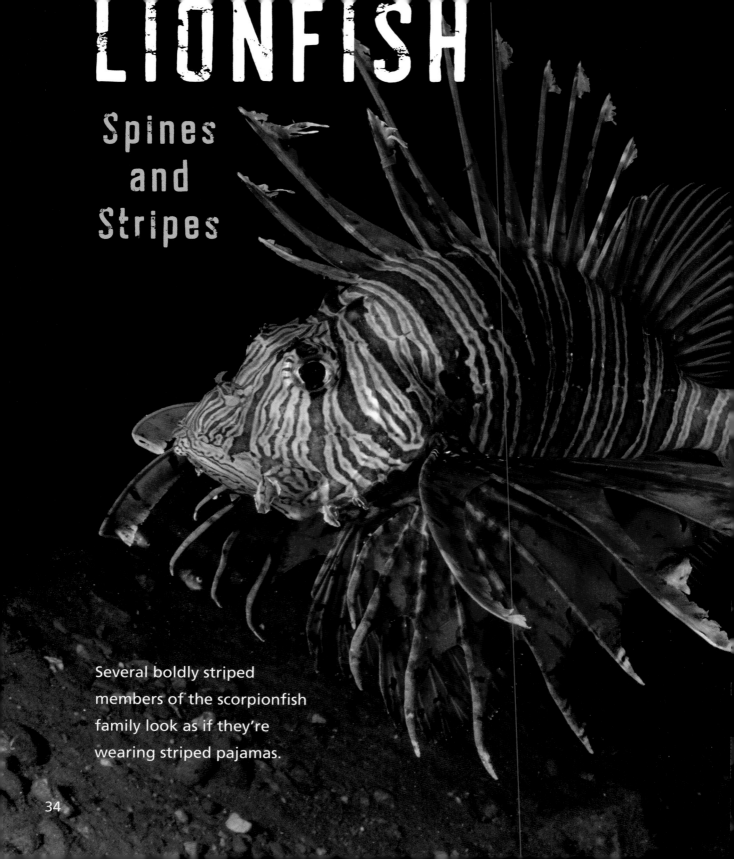

LIONFISH

Spines and Stripes

Several boldly striped
members of the scorpionfish
family look as if they're
wearing striped pajamas.

Lionfish swim above the seafloor, spreading their fin spines like Chinese fans. When challenged by intruders—including unwary scuba divers—a lionfish will slowly turn its needle-like, venomous dorsal spines toward the unwelcome visitor. Divers observing this behavior should back off.

W NATURE
WORKS

INVASIVE SPECIES

An invasive species is a non-native plant, animal, or other living thing whose negativ[e] [im]pact on a local habitat is greater than any positive value it may provide. In the 1990s, th[e] lionfish, a native of the Pacific and Indian oceans, turned up in Florida's coastal waters. T[oday] this invasive species is common throughout the Caribbean Sea and north to Cape Hat[teras,] North Carolina. Juvenile lionfish have been spotted as far north as Rhode Island.

How did it get so far from home? Fish biologists think that some escaped from o[ne or] more aquariums near a Florida beach during the floods caused by Hurricane Andr[ew in] 1992. A serious threat to the North Atlantic fish it devours, the lionfish reminds aqua[rium] hobbyists not to release pet fish into the wild. When an invasive species enters a new [ter-]ritory without its native predators, parasites, and diseases, it can outcompete local fis[h and] disrupt an entire ecosystem.

STRIPED EEL CATFISH

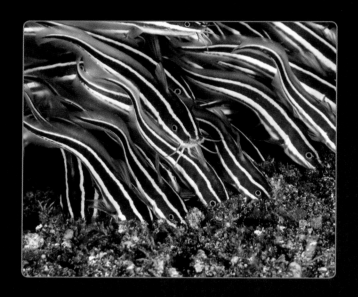

Schools of this catfish look harmless as they maneuver in tight formations near sandy ocean bottoms, but they're armed with highly venomous spines on their dorsal and front side fins. More than 750 catfish species in salt and fresh waters protect themselves with spines and venom glands.

STRIPED FANGBLENNY

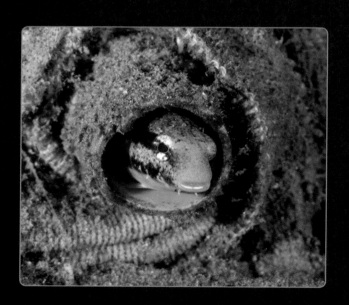

When this blenny bites, venom flows along grooves on each of two long teeth in its lower jaw and into the wound. Fish-eating predators steer clear of this small fish with bold black, white, and yellow stripes and its nearly identical yet non-venomous cousin, the striped fangblenny mimic.

NIGEL'S ONE-JAWED EEL

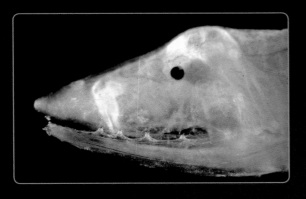

What could be creepier than this small, predatory ocean fish (not a true eel) that attacks its prey with a single venomous fang attached to the roof of its mouth? It has no upper jaw. There's no need for nightmares about this venomous beast, though. It's only 2 inches (51 mm) long, and it lives at such cold, dark depths that you are never likely to get near one unless you are in a submarine.

STARGAZER FISH

The stargazer has both defensive and offensive weapon systems. Lying on its belly on a sandy seabed with its eyes gazing up, it protects itself with a pair of venomous spines, one on each side of its body. Meanwhile, using special electric organs, it generates an invisible field that detects small fish, which it turns into fast food.

THE BANDED SEA KRAIT
Real Sea Serpents

In the Pacific Ocean, near the islands of Fiji, a snake called a sea krait swims into a narrow cave within a coral reef.

Inside the cave, a voracious moray eel guards its home. This dangerous predator can strike like a lightning bolt. A side-to-side wiggling of its body exerts force against the water around it, generating a reactive force that propels the moray forward with power and speed.

A moray eel guards its lair.

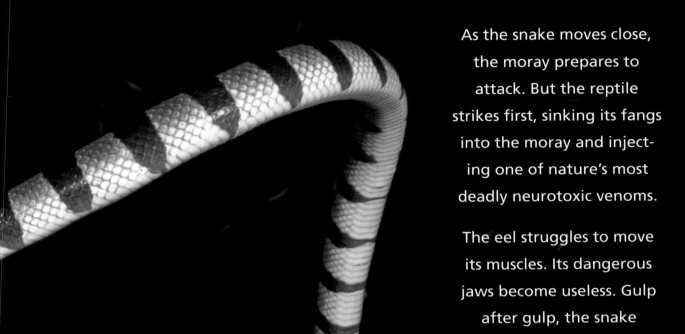

Its jaws house rows of sharp teeth, behind which is a second set of jaws that will lunge forward, pulling captured food back into the animal's throat.

As the snake moves close, the moray prepares to attack. But the reptile strikes first, sinking its fangs into the moray and injecting one of nature's most deadly neurotoxic venoms.

The eel struggles to move its muscles. Its dangerous jaws become useless. Gulp after gulp, the snake swallows its meal.

HOW NATURE WORKS

DIVING WITH SEA SNAKES

Sea snake venom is among the most powerful yet discovered. Fortunately, with their small mouths and tiny fangs, these snakes can't easily bite a human, and they are almost never aggressive when left alone. Still, smart divers keep a respectful distance from these beautiful reptiles.

VENOMOUS SEA CREATURES
Up Close and Personal

Venom production has evolved over and over in sea creatures. For example, a team at the University of Kansas Biodiversity Institute found that venom systems have evolved independently eighteen times among the nearly 3,000 venomous fish species the team studied: four times in cartilaginous fishes, once in eels, once in catfishes, and twelve times in spiny-rayed fishes. When evolution arrives at the same solution so many times, we can surmise that it must offer a powerful adaptive advantage.

The more than two million animal species on Earth are grouped into more than 30 phyla (major groupings of organisms) so far. Only ten of these include land-dwelling species, perhaps because multicellular animals evolved in the sea some 600 million years ago but didn't begin to invade the land until about 400 million years ago. There has been more time for marine phyla to evolve, and not all of them have been able to make the transition to land.

So, although there are many more venomous animal *species* on land than in the sea, there are more venomous *phyla* in the sea: six in the sea versus only two on land. In order of increasing evolutionary complexity, the venomous marine phyla are cnidarians (for example, sea anemones), mollusks (for example, cone snails), annelids (for example, bristle worms), arthropods (for example, remipedes), echinoderms (for example, fire urchins), and chordates (for example, scorpionfish).

Here are the venomous species in this book, listed by phylum:

Cnidarians (nye-DAIR-ee-uns)

Northern Red Sea Anemone

Scientific name: *Urticina felina*

Range: *Arctic to Cape Cod and Alaska to California*

Height: Up to 5 inches (13 cm)

What it eats: Crabs, shrimp, sea jellies, sea urchins, and small fish

Hydra

Scientific name: *Hydra* spp.

Length: Up to 0.6 inch (15 mm) not including extended tentacles

Range: Temperate and tropical fresh waters worldwide

What it eats: Zooplankton

Anemones symbiotic with clownfish

Scientific names: Ten anemone species in the following genera host clownfish: *Heteractis, Stichodactyla, Entacmaea, Macrodactyla, Cryptodendrum.*

Diameter: 8 inches (20 cm) to 3.3 feet (1 meter)

Range: Indo-Pacific

What they eat: Fish, zooplankton, shrimp, and other small crustaceans

Star Coral

Scientific name: *Montastrea* spp.

Diameter of colonies: Up to 13 feet (4 meters)

Range: Tropical and subtropical seas worldwide

What it eats: Zooplankton

Lion's Mane Jelly

Scientific name: *Cyanea capillata*

Diameter: Up to 8 feet (2.4 m); length of tentacles up to 100 feet (30 m) or more

Range: Arctic to Florida and Alaska to Washington

What it eats: Fishes, moon jellies, crustaceans, and zooplankton

Upside-Down Jelly

Scientific name: *Cassiopeia* spp.

Diameter: Up to 12 inches (30 cm)

Range: Tropical and subtropical seas worldwide

What it eats: Zooplankton and nutrients produced by internal zooxanthellae

Box Jelly

Scientific name: *Chironex fleckeri*

Diameter: Up to 11 inches (28 cm), length of tentacles up to 10 feet (3 m)

Range: Northern Australia to New Guinea,

Vietnam, and the Philippines

What it eats: Fish and shrimp

Irukandji Box Jelly

Scientific name: *Carukia barnesi* and about 15 other species

Diameter: Up to 1 inch (25 mm); length of tentacles up to 3.3 feet (1m)

Range: Northern Australia

What it eats: Zooplankton

Mollusks

Greater Blue-Ringed Octopus

Scientific name: *Hapalochlaena lunulata*

Arm span: Up to 8 inches (20 cm)

Range: Indo-Pacific

What it eats: Crabs, shrimp, and small fishes

Textile Cone Snail

Scientific name: *Conus textile*

Length: Up to 4 inches (10 cm)

Range: Indo-Pacific

What it eats: Snails

Magician's Cone Snail

Scientific name: *Conus magus*

Length: Up to 3.7 inches (9 cm)

Range: Indo-Pacific

What it eats: Fish

Chinese Dragon Sea Slug

Scientific name: *Pteraeolidia ianthina*

Length: Up to 4 inches (10 cm)

Range: Indo-Pacific

What it eats: Hydroids

Annelids

Bloodworm

Scientific name: *Glycera dibranchiata*

Length: Up to 10 inches (25 cm)

Range: Atlantic and Pacific coasts of North America, Gulf of Mexico, and Mediterranean Sea

What it eats: Crustaceans and detritus

Bearded Fireworm

Scientific name: *Hermodice carunculata*

Length: Up to 13 inches (33 cm)

Range: Caribbean Sea and Gulf of Mexico

What it eats: Coral, anemones, and crustaceans

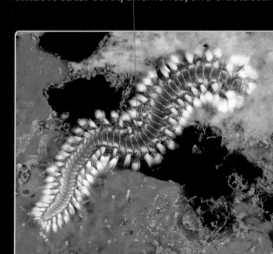

Arthropods

Blind Remipede (REM-eye-peed)
Scientific name: *Speleonectes lucayensis*

Length: Up to 1.6 inches (4 cm)

Range: Bahama Islands

What it eats: Shrimp and other crustaceans

Echinoderms

Flower Urchin
Scientific name: *Toxopneustes pileolus*

Diameter: Up to 6 inches (15 cm)

Range: Indo-Pacific

What it eats: Algae and detritus

Fire Urchin
Scientific name: *Asthenosoma varium*

Diameter: Up to 8 inches (20 cm)

Range: Indo-Pacific

What it eats: Algae and invertebrates

Crown of Thorns Sea Star
Scientific name: *Toxopneustes pileolus*

Diameter: Up to 14 inches (36 cm)

Range: Indo-Pacific and Pacific coast of Central America

What it eats: Coral polyps

Chordates

Bluespotted Stingray
Scientific name: *Dasyatis kuhlii*

Length: Up to 27 inches (69 cm)

Range: Indo-Pacific

What it eats: Crabs and shrimp

Scorpionfish
Family: Scorpaenidae

Range: Tropical and temperate seas worldwide

Length: 6 to 14 inches (15 to 36 cm)

What it eats: Fish and invertebrates

Reef Stonefish
Scientific name: *Synanceia verrucosa*

Range: Indo-Pacific

Length: Up to 16 inches (41 cm)

What it eats: Fish and invertebrates

Red Lionfish
Scientific name: *Pterois volitans*

Range: Native to Indo-Pacific; invasive in western Atlantic

Length: Up to 15 inches (38 cm)

What it eats: Fish, shrimp, crabs, and a variety of invertebrates

Palette Surgeonfish

Scientific name: *Paracanthurus hepatus*

Range: Indo-Pacific

Length: Up to 12 inches (30 cm)

What it eats: Invertebrates including zooplankton

Striped Eel Catfish

Scientific name: *Plotosus lineatus*

Range: Indo-Pacific

Length: Up to 10 inches (25 cm)

What it eats: Crustaceans, mollusks, and worms

Striped Fangblenny

Scientific name: *Meiacanthus grammistes*

Range: Indo-Pacific

Length: Up to 3.7 inches (9.5 cm)

What it eats: Zooplankton

Nigel's One-Jawed Eel

Scientific name: *Monognathus nigeli*

Range: Known from the eastern North Atlantic
t depths of 2,000 to 5,400 meters; full extent of
ange unknown

Length: Up to 2.3 inches (6 cm)

What it eats: Most likely shrimp, but little is
nown about its diet

Whitemargin Stargazer

Scientific name: *Uranoscopus sulphureus*

Range: Indo-Pacific

Length: Up to 18 inches (46 cm)

What it eats: Fish and shrimp

Banded Sea Krait

Scientific name: *Laticauda colubrina*

Range: Indo-Pacific

Length: Males up to 30 inches (76 cm); females
to 50 inches (1.3 meters)

What it eats: Eels

Although venomous sea creatures will defend
themselves, they are easy to avoid. Learn all you
can about these fascinating animals and observ
them from a safe distance. It is very unlikely tha
a venomous marine animal will ever seriously
injure you.

A Timeline of Earth's History

Scientists think that Earth formed 4.6 billion years ago, and the first single-celled organisms appeared about 3.5 billion years ago. But nearly 3 billion more years elapsed before organisms with more than one cell appeared, some 600 million years ago. Sponges and comb jellies were among those first multicelled organisms, and they are still around today.

The top timeline covers all of Earth history. The bottom timeline expands the Phanerozoic eon, which began about 541 million years ago.

EARTH TIMELINE

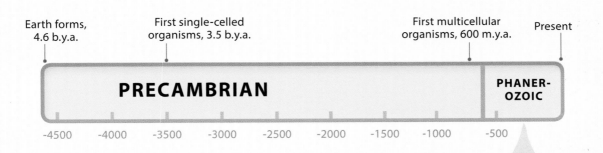

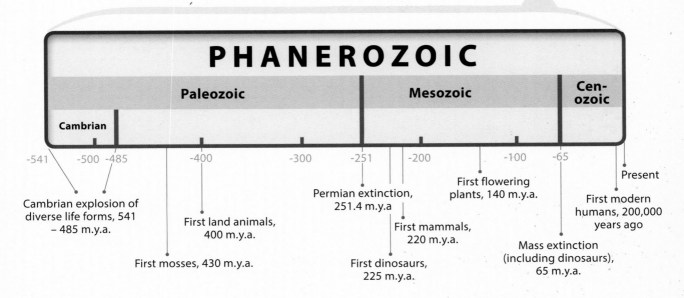

DIVE DEEPER!
Learn More About Venomous Marine Creatures

Online

www.venomdoc.com
Bryan Grieg Fry from the University of Queensland, Australia, shares discoveries about venomous fish.

www.montereybayaquarium.org/animals-and-exhibits/animal-guide;
www.aquariumofpacific.org/onlinelearningcenter/species/
Profiles of a wide variety of venomous fishes, jellies, coral, and other marine animals.

Books

Amazing Jellies: Jewels of the Sea, by Elizabeth Tayntor Gowell, Bunker Hill Publishing, 2004.

The Ancestor's Tale: A Pilgrimage to the Dawn of Evolution, by Richard Dawkins and Yan Wong, Houghton Mifflin Company, 2004.

Coral Reef Animals of the Indo-Pacific, by Terrence M. Gossliner, David W. Behrens, and Gary C. Williams, Sea Challengers, 1996.

Dangerous Marine Animals: That Bite, Sting, Shock, or Are Non-Edible, by Bruce W. Halstead, by Schiffer Publishing, 1979.

Deadly Kingdom: The Book of Dangerous Animals, by Gordon Grice, The Dial Press, 2010.

Poisonous and Venomous Marine Animals of the World, by Bruce W. Halstead, The Darwin Press, 1978.

Poisonous Marine Animals, by Findlay E. Russell, T.F.H. Publications, 1971.

Spineless: The Science of Jellyfish and the Art of Growing a Backbone, by Juli Berwald, Riverhead Books, 2017.

Stung! On Jellyfish Blooms and the Future of the Ocean, by Lisa-ann Gershwin, University of Chicago Press, 2013.

Sustaining Life: How Human Health Depends on Biodiversity, edited by Eric Chivian and Aaron Bernstein, Oxford University Press, 2008.

GLOSSARY

aposematic *(ah-puh-suh-MAT-ic)* coloration: Bold protective colors and patterns that warn or repel predators.

batrachotoxin *(ba-tra-ko-TOX-in)*: A powerful toxin found in certain frogs, beetles, and birds.

cerata *(ser-AH-tuh)*: Outgrowths of the digestive system on the surface of certain nudibranchs (sea slugs).

cnidocytes *(NYE-doe-sites)*: Specialized cells in anemones and other cnidarians containing nematocysts.

epithelium *(ep-uh-THEE-lee-um)*: Tissue that forms the outer surface of an animal's body.

nematocysts *(nem-AT-oh-sists)*: Specialized organelles found in the cells of anemones and other cnidarians. Some kinds of nematocysts can sting.

neurotoxin *(nur-oh-TOX-in)*: A poison or venom that affects the nervous system.

nudibranch *(NEW-duh-brank)*: A marine, soft-bodied gastropod mollusk having no shell in its adult stage. Nudibranchs are often called sea slugs.

organelle *(or-gan-ELL)*: A specialized structure within a cell.

pedicellariae *(ped-uh-sell-AIR-ee-uh)*: Defensive pincerlike structures on the surface of echinoderms.

peptide *(PEP-tide)*: A small protein consisting of between two to fifty amino acids.

phylum *(FIE-lum)*: A major group of organisms classified below kingdom and above class.

polyp *(PAHL-up)*: An individual cnidarian animal such as a coral, anemone, or the stationary stage of a sea jelly.

proboscis *(pro-BAH-sis)*: In the case of worms, this is an extendible part of the mouth structure.

protein *(PRO-teen)*: An organic compound having one or more long chains of amino acids.

tetrodotoxin *(te-trow-duh-TOX-in)*: A powerful neurotoxin found in certain species of pufferfish.

toxin *(TOX-in)*: A poison or venom produced by animals, plants, and other living things.

venom *(VE-nom)*: A toxin that is injected into predators or prey using stingers, spines, or other tissue-penetrating structures.

ziconotide *(zie-CON-oh-tide)*: A bioactive peptide pain reliever inspired by a peptide found in the cone snail *Conus magus*.

zooplankton *(ZOH-uh-plank-ton)*: An animal that drifts with water currents. Typically the word refers to microscopic organisms, although large sea jellies are also considered zooplankton.

zooxanthellae *(zoh-uh-zan-THELL-ee)*: A plantlike microorganism in the genus Symbiodinium that lives in the tissues of reef-building corals and other animals.

PAUL ERICKSON creates websites, exhibits, guides, and videos for zoos, museums, and aquariums nationwide. He has authored or co-authored numerous magazine articles and three books about undersea life. His book *The Pier at the End of the World* (Tilbury House) was named an Outstanding Science Trade Book of 2016 by the National Science Teachers Association.

ANDREW MARTINEZ specializes in images of the undersea world and is the author and photographer of *Marine Life of the North Atlantic*. He travels the world to photograph sea life, and was the photographer for *The Pier at the End of the World*.

HOW NATURE WORKS

HOW NATURE WORKS books don't just catalog the natural world in beautiful photographs. They seek to understand why nature functions as it does. They ask questions, and they encourage readers to ask more. They explore nature's mysteries, sharing what we know and celebrating what we have yet to discover. Other HOW NATURE WORKS books include:

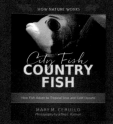

Catching Air:
Taking the Leap with Gliding Animals
Sneed B. Collard III
978-0-8848-496-7

City Fish, Country Fish:
How Fish Adapt to Tropical Seas and Cold Oceans
Mary M. Cerullo
978-0-88448-529-2

Extreme Survivors:
Animals That Time Forgot
Kimberly Ridley
978-0-88448-500-1

One Iguana, Two Iguanas:
A Story of Accident, Natural Selection, and Evolution
Sneed B. Collard III
978-0-88448-649-7